Instructions on page 37.

Cushions

Instructions on page 52

Instructions on page 41.

Instructions on page 35.

Instructions on page 58.

Instructions on page 86

Tablecloths

Instructions on page 82.

Instructions on page 40.

Instructions on page 68.

Instructions on pages 33 & 34.

Instructions on page 63.

Instructions on page 60.

Instructions on page 49.

Pictures

Instructions on page 45.

Albums

Instructions on page 51.

30

Instructions on page 78.

Instructions on page 63.

●Instructions

Materials: 55cm (21 ⅝″) square of Beige Zweigart art.3707 Hertarette ［10cm (4″) square = 32.5 meshes square］; DMC six-strand embroidery floss No.25: 5 skeins of Antique blue (930), 4 skeins each of Antique blue (932) and Azure blue (775), 2 skeins each of Moss green (470, 937) and Pistachio green (320), 1 skein each of Magenta rose (963), Peony rose (957), Rose pink (961), Old rose (3350), Raspberry red (3685), Parma violet (209, 211), Plum (550, 553), Moss green (471) and Ivy green (500), a little each of Saffron (725) and Golden yellow (780); 166cm (65 ⅜″) Blue-gray braid 1.5cm (⅝″) wide, 166cm (65 ⅜″) Beige bias tape 1.5cm (⅝″) wide.

Finished size: See chart.

Instructions: After matching the center of fabric and pattern, embroider design referring to chart A with 6-strand embroidery floss. Cut fabric to instructed size. Bind edges with bias tape, and stitch braid.

Finished Diagram

Bind edges with bias tape, and stitch braid on Front.

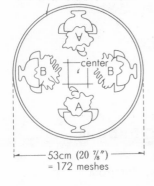

— 53cm (20 ⅞″) — = 172 meshes

Ⅱ	= 961
✕	= 775
◯	= 932
◉	= 930
⌊	= 211
◪	= 209
◲	= 553
◪	= 550
T	= 471
△	= 470
◓	= 937
Ⅰ	= 320
▲	= 500
⊞	= 725

8 meshes

center

One square = 1×1 mesh

See next page for chart B.

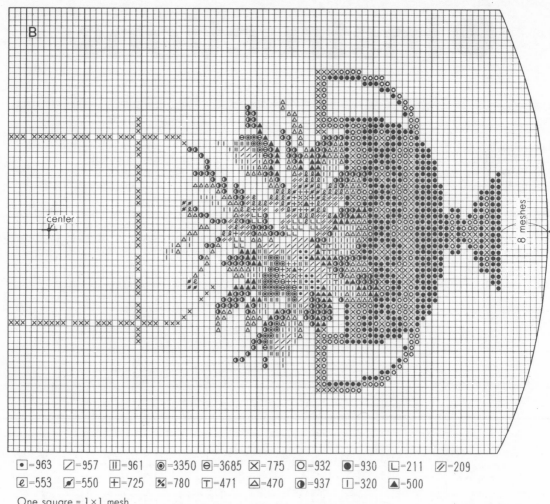

●=963 ⧹=957 ‖=961 ◉=3350 ⊖=3685 ☒=775 ◯=932 ⬤=930 L=211 ⧸=209

ℓ=553 ⬗=550 ⊞=725 ⊠=780 T=471 △=470 ◐=937 ⊡=320 ▲=500

One square = 1×1 mesh

Doily ——————————— Shown on page 18.

Materials: 72cm by 51cm (28 ³/₈″×20 ¹/₁₆″) of Beige
Zweigart art.3707 Hertarette [10cm (4″) square = 32.
5 meshes square] ; DMC six-strand embroidery floss
No.25: 4 skeins of Antique blue (932), 2 skeins of
Antique blue (930), 1 skein each of Azure blue (775),
Plum (550, 553), Parma violet (209, 211), Moss green
(470, 471, 500, 937), Pistachio green (320), Saffron
(725) and Magenta rose (961); 214cm (84 ¼″) bias
tape of 1.8cm (³/₄″)-wide.
Finished size: 63cm by 44cm. (24 ³/₄″×17 ³/₈″).
Instructions: Cut out fabric to size, and embroider as
chart A of DOILY using 6 strands of floss. Turn back
allowance and finish edges with bias tape.

Finished Diagram

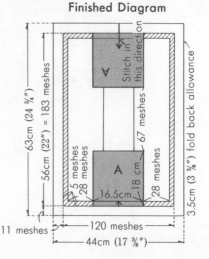

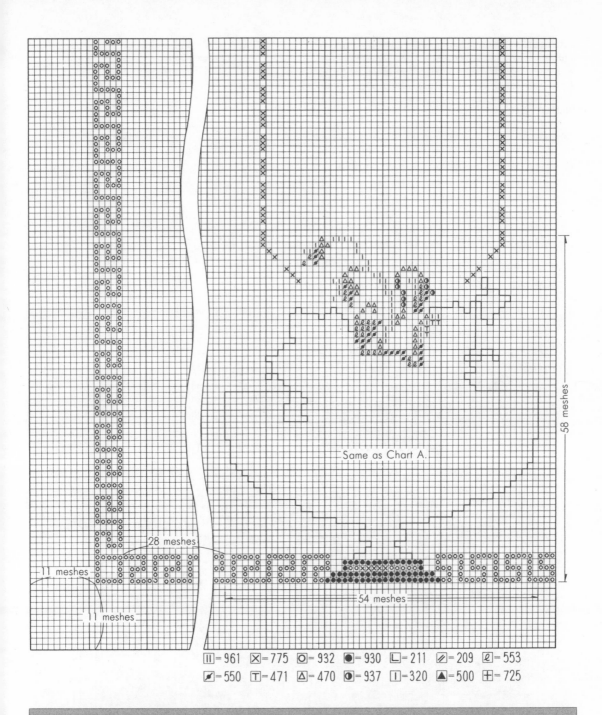

Ⅱ = 961	☒ = 775	◯ = 932	● = 930	L = 211	✐ = 209	ℓ = 553
✐ = 550	T = 471	△ = 470	◐ = 937	Ⅰ = 320	▲ = 500	⊞ = 725

Cushion ──────────── Shown on page 5.

Materials: 95cm by 51cm (37 ⅜″×20″) of Beige Zweigart art.3970 Diamant Aida [10cm (4″) square = 28 meshes square] ; DMC six-strand embroidery floss No.25: 1 skein each of Moss green (937, 470, 471), Ivy green (501) and Almond green (502, 503), 0. 5 skeins each of Plum (553, 554), Episcopal purple (718), Almond green (504), Tangerine yellow (741, 742, 743), Saffron (727), Old gold (676, 680, 729), Royal blue (797), Sèvres blue (798, 799, 820), Ger- anium red (349, 350, 351, 817) and Flame red (606); 720cm (283 ½″) long brown cord of 0.7cm (¼″) in diameter; 40cm (15 ¾″) zipper; 105cm by 55cm (41 ⅜″ × 21 ⅝″) of fabric for inner bag as pad; 500g (18 oz) Polyester fiberfill.
Finished size: 47cm (18 ½″) square.

Instructions: Embroider according to chart using 6 strands. After completing design, sew pieces together with right sides facing. Sew zipper in center of Back. Twist together 3 cords and sew along edges. Stuff inner bag, 50cm (19 ⅝″) square, and cover with finished outer bag.

Arrangement

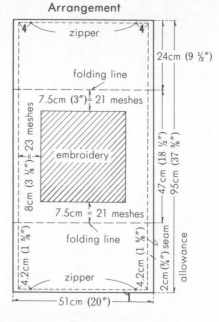

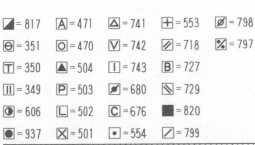

◪ = 817	Ⓐ = 471	◭ = 741	⊞ = 553	⊘ = 798
⊖ = 351	Ⓞ = 470	Ⓥ = 742	▨ = 718	⊠ = 797
⊤ = 350	▲ = 504	Ⅱ = 743	Ⓑ = 727	
Ⅲ = 349	Ⓟ = 503	◩ = 680	◩ = 729	
◑ = 606	Ⓛ = 502	Ⓒ = 676	■ = 820	
● = 937	⊠ = 501	• = 554	◺ = 799	

One square = 1×1 mesh

center

31cm (12 ¼″) = 87 meshes

Materials: 51cm by 38cm. (20 $\frac{1}{16}$"
× 15") of Beige Zweigart art.3707
Hertarette [10cm (4") square = 32.
5 meshes square] ; DMC six-strand
embroidery floss No.25: 2 skeins
each of Parakeet green (904), Laurel green (989), Scarab green
(3348) and Lemon yellow (445), 1
skein each of Geranium red (948,
754, 351), Sage green (3012), Yellow green (734), Sage green (3013),
Episcopal purple (718), Parma
violet (211, 209), Indian red (3041,
3042), Buttercup yellow (444),
Lemon yellow (307), Canary yellow (972), Umber (433), Chestnut
(407, 950), Golden yellow (782),
Scarlet (498), Poppy (666) and
White, a little each of Orange
(970), Flame red (608), Ash gray
(415) and Forget-me-not blue
(827); 100cm by 110cm (39 $\frac{3}{8}$" ×
43 $\frac{3}{8}$") of Red velvet; 52cm (20 $\frac{1}{2}$")
zipper; 95cm by 62cm. (37 $\frac{3}{8}$" ×
24 $\frac{3}{8}$") of cotton for a inner bag;
850g (30 oz) polyester fiberfill;
600cm (236") heavy yarn.
Finished size: See chart.
Instructions: Cut fabric according
to chart. Cross stitch with 6
strands and straight stitch with 3
strands. Cut out velvet according
to chart. Gather front piece and
run yarn through casing. Sew
pieces with right sides together,
and sew zipper onto Back. To
make inner cushion, fill bag with
stuffing. Bag should be made ap-
prox.3cm bigger than finished size.

See next page for design.

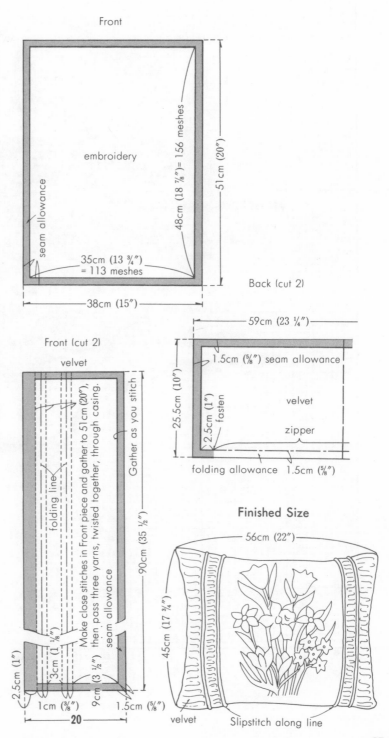

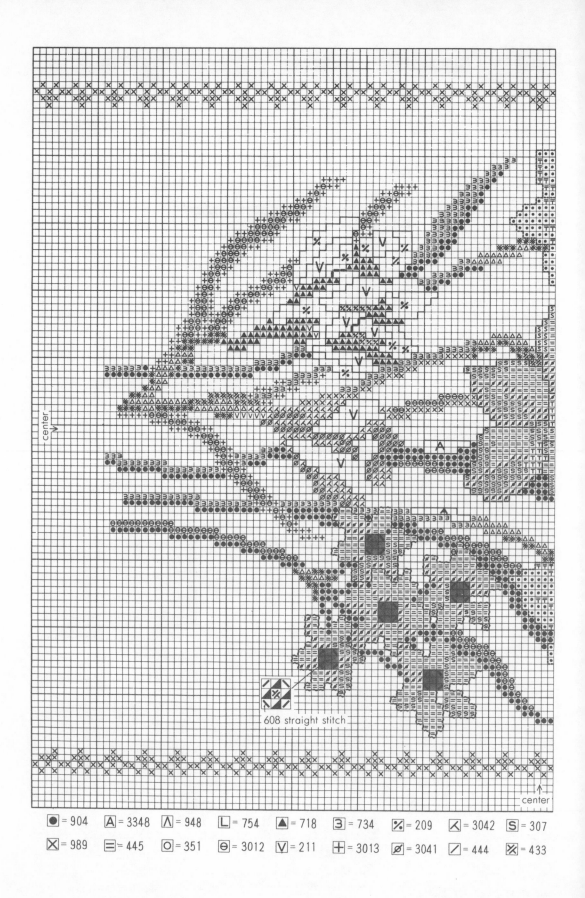

608 straight stitch

● = 904   Ａ = 3348   Λ = 948   Ｌ = 754   ▲ = 718   Ɜ = 734   ％ = 209   ⋋ = 3042   Ｓ = 307

☒ = 989   ＝ = 445   Ｏ = 351   ⊖ = 3012   Ⅴ = 211   ＋ = 3013   ∅ = 3041   ／ = 444   ⊠ = 433

433 straight stitch

One square = 1×1 mesh

△ = 407 ▨ = 666 T = 782 ◑ = 970 ⊤ = 415

※ = 950 • = white ◎ = 498 ◣ = 608 ▨ = 972

⌐ = 718 ⌐ = 827
⌐ = 782 ⌐ = 444 } line stitch

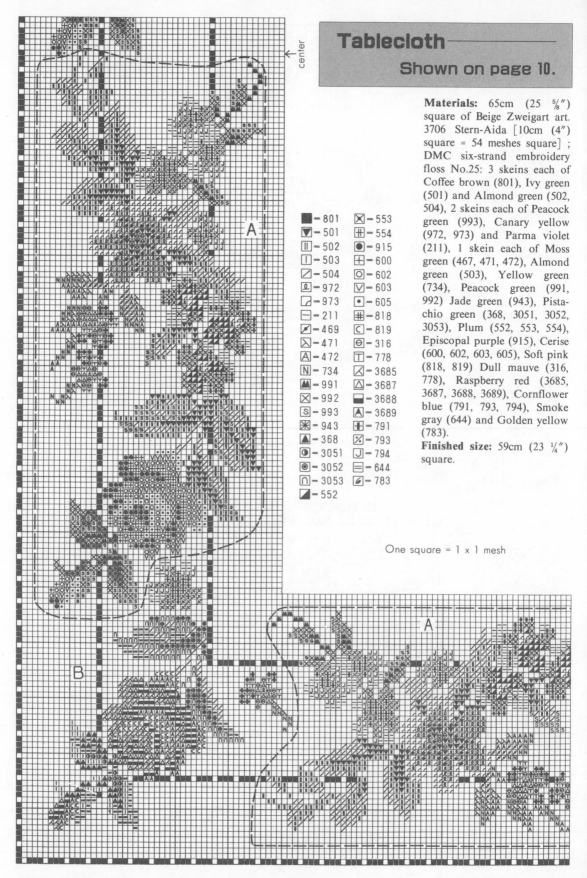

center

Materials: 65cm (25 ⅝″) square of Beige Zweigart art. 3706 Stern-Aida [10cm (4″) square = 54 meshes square] ; DMC six-strand embroidery floss No.25: 3 skeins each of Coffee brown (801), Ivy green (501) and Almond green (502, 504), 2 skeins each of Peacock green (993), Canary yellow (972, 973) and Parma violet (211), 1 skein each of Moss green (467, 471, 472), Almond green (503), Yellow green (734), Peacock green (991, 992) Jade green (943), Pistachio green (368, 3051, 3052, 3053), Plum (552, 553, 554), Episcopal purple (915), Cerise (600, 602, 603, 605), Soft pink (818, 819) Dull mauve (316, 778), Raspberry red (3685, 3687, 3688, 3689), Cornflower blue (791, 793, 794), Smoke gray (644) and Golden yellow (783).
Finished size: 59cm (23 ¼″) square.

■ – 801	⊠ – 553		
▼ – 501	⊞ – 554		
‖ – 502	● – 915		
Ⅰ – 503	⊞ – 600		
╱ – 504	○ – 602		
ℓ – 972	∨ – 603		
╱ – 973	• – 605		
⊟ – 211	⊞ – 818		
◪ – 469	© – 819		
⊠ – 471	⊖ – 316		
△ – 472	⊤ – 778		
N – 734	⊠ – 3685		
▲ – 991	△ – 3687		
⊠ – 992	■ – 3688		
S – 993	▲ – 3689		
✳ – 943	⊞ – 791		
▲ – 368	⊿ – 793		
◑ – 3051	J – 794		
◎ – 3052	⊟ – 644		
⋂ – 3053	⬛ – 783		
◪ – 552			

One square = 1 x 1 mesh

Instructions: Embroider with 3 strands of floss according to chart. After completing the design, fold back allowance along line, and miter corners to finish.

Materials: 90cm by 46.5cm (35 ½″ × 18 ¼″) Beige Zweigart art.3706 Stern-Aida [10cm (4″) square = 54 meshes square]; DMC six-strands of embroidery floss No.25: 3 skeins of Parakeet green (906), 2 skeins each of Parakeet green (904) and Umber (433), 1 skein each of Moss green (472), Canary yellow (972), Tangerine Yellow (743, 745, 740), Scarlet (816), Geranium red (349, 351), Cerise (603, 605), Soft pink (818), Scabious violet (327), Plum (553, 554), Indigo (939), Cornflower blue (917) and White; 95 by 50cm (37 ⅜″ × 19 ⅝″) fabric for Inner bag; 40cm (15 ¾″) zipper; 500g (18oz) polyester fiberfill.

Finished size: 42.5cm by 43cm (16 ¾″ × 16 ⅞″).

Instructions: Cross stitch using 4 strands of floss and line stitch with 1 strand according to chart. With right sides together, sew fabric along folding line, making gentle curve.

Attach zipper to center of Back piece. Stuff inner bag, 45 cm by 46cm (17 ¾″ × 18 ⅛″), and cover with finished outer cushion.

Arrangement

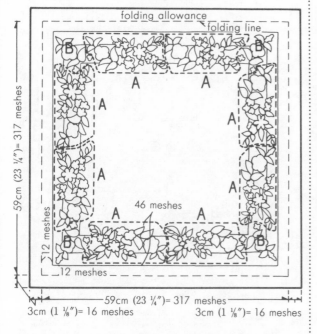

Arrangement

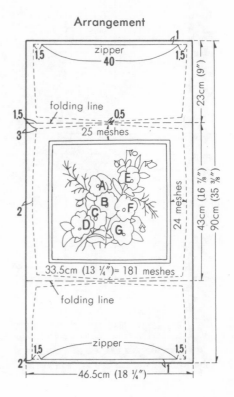

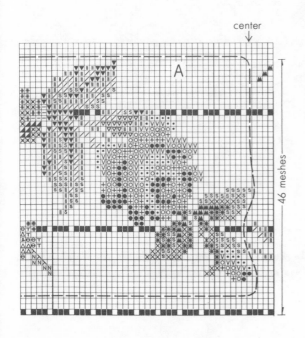

See next page for design.

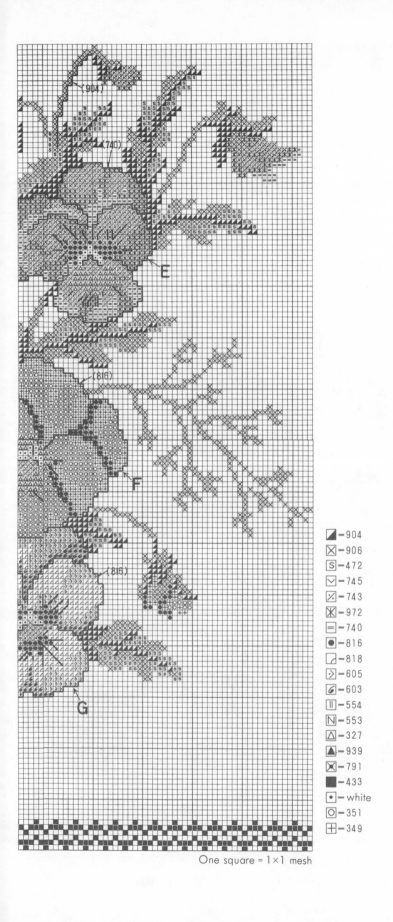

One square = 1×1 mesh

Symbol	Color
◣	–904
✕	–906
S	–472
∨	–745
◿	–743
✕	–972
=	–740
●	–816
◿	–818
⊳	–605
◢	–603
‖	–554
N	–553
△	–327
▲	–939
✕	–791
■	–433
••	–white
O	–351
+	–349

Line stitch in center of flowers with colors directed below.

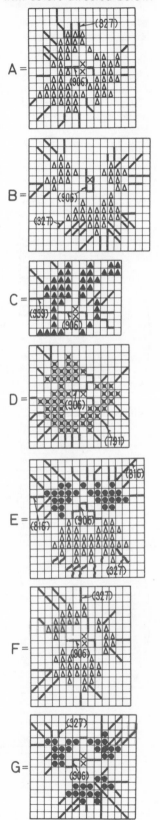

43

Materials: 85cm by 8.5cm (33 ½″×3 ⅜″) of White Zweigart art.3609 Belfast [10cm (4″) square = 122 meshes square]; DMC six-strand embroidery floss No. 25: 1 skein of White, 0.5 skeins each of Golden yellow (782, 783), Saffron (725, 727), Sky blue (518, 519) and Geranium red (352), a little of each Yellow green (730, 733), Copper green (829, 831), Sky blue (517), Scarlet (498), Geranium red (350) and Black (310); 80cm by 18cm (31 ½″×3 ⅛″) White glue lining. (For 5 pcs. set as shown.)

Finished size: 8cm (3 ⅛″) in diameter.
Instructions: Embroider each front piece using 2 strands for cross stitch and 1 strand for line stitch, as directed on chart. After completing design, put glue lining on wrong side of each piece, as well as on wrong side of Back.
Complete glass mats by cutting out materials according to chart.

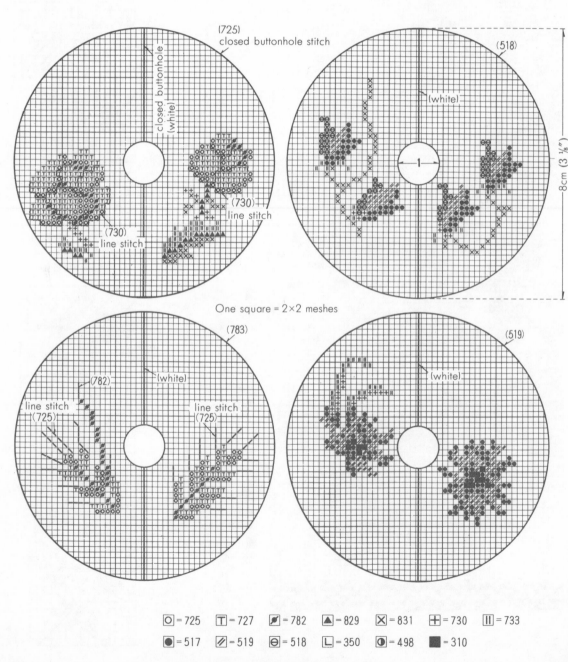

◯ = 725	T = 727	◪ = 782	▲ = 829	✕ = 831	✚ = 730	Ⅲ = 733
● = 517	▨ = 519	◒ = 518	L = 350	◑ = 498	■ = 310	

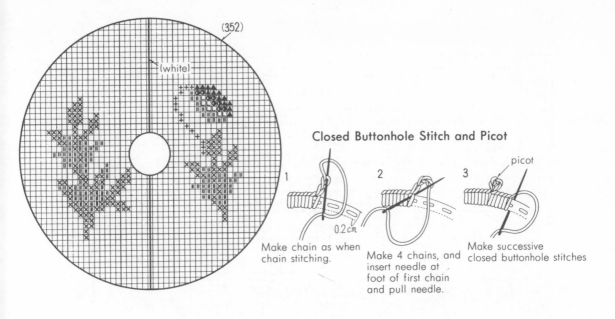

(352)

(white)

Closed Buttonhole Stitch and Picot

1   Make chain as when chain stitching.

0.2 cm

2   Make 4 chains, and insert needle at foot of first chain and pull needle.

3   picot   Make successive closed buttonhole stitches

How to Complete Mats

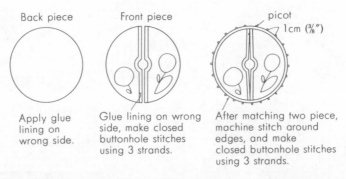

Back piece

Apply glue lining on wrong side.

Front piece

Glue lining on wrong side, make closed buttonhole stitches using 3 strands.

picot — 1cm (³/₈″)

After matching two piece, machine stitch around edges, and make closed buttonhole stitches using 3 strands.

Picture ——————————— Shown on page 27.

Materials: 38cm by 29cm (15″×11 ³/₈″) Beige Zweigart art.3706 Stern-Aida [10cm (4″) square = 54 square meshes]; DMC six-strand embroidery floss No. 25, 1 strand of Scarab green (3348, 3345), Moss green (703, 472), Yellow green (732), Green (3053), Terra-cotta (355, 356, 758), Parakeet green (905, 907), Chestnut (407), Beige green (839), Buttercup yellow (444), Lemon yellow (445), Ash gray (413), Beige (3023), Beaver gray (647), Old gold (676), Copper green (832), Forget-me-not blue (828, 813), Black (310), Cream (746) and White, a little of Flame red (606); Picture frame.

Finished size: See chart.

Instructions: After matching center of pattern and fabric, use 3 strands for cross and half cross stitches, and 2 strands for line stitch.

Frame work when completed.

See next page for design.

Finished Diagram

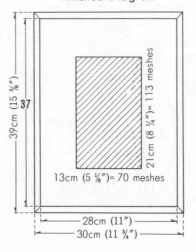

39cm (15 ³/₈″)

37

1

21cm (8 ¼″)= 113 meshes

13cm (5 ⅛″)= 70 meshes

28cm (11″)

30cm (11 ¾″)

(839) line stitch

(310) line stitch

(413) line stitch

(3345) line stitch

P

center

center

One square = 1 x 1 mesh

cross stitch
half cross stitch

a D	=	703
T E	=	905
⅄ 3	=	732
7 h	=	3023
• B	=	white
− P	=	828
‖	=	472
≡	=	907
✕	=	3345
∧	=	3053
L	=	355
V	=	356
S	=	758
Y	=	407
▲	=	839
◐	=	444
◑	=	445
✛	=	647
A	=	676
C	=	832
✎	=	3348
⁄⁄	=	813
●	=	310
I	=	746
◉	=	606

● Doily

Materials: 74cm (29 ⅛″) square of Beige Zweigart art.3707 Hertarette [10cm (4″) square = 32.5 meshes square]; DMC six-strand embroidery floss No.25: 9 skeins of Parakeet green (907), 8 skeins of Parakeet green (905), 4 skeins each of Peacock green (991), Emerald green (911) and Tangerine yellow (740), 3 skeins each of Geranium red (350), Umber gold (977), Buttercup yellow (444), Peacock green (992) and Emerald green (954), 2 skeins each of White, Parma violet (209, 211), Pistachio green (368), Mahogany (400), Lemon yellow (445), Cerise (601), Soft pink (899, 776), Royal blue (797), Cornflower blue (792) and Forget-me-not blue (826), 1 skein each of Black (310), Ash gray (318, 415), Turkey red (321), Poppy (666), Scabious violet (327) and Plum (554), a little of Tangerine yellow (742).

Finished size: 68cm (26 ¾″) square.

Instructions: Cross stitch with 12 strands of floss and line stitch with 3 strands, as directed on chart. After completing design, turn back allowance and stitch edges. Miter corners to finish.

Arrangement

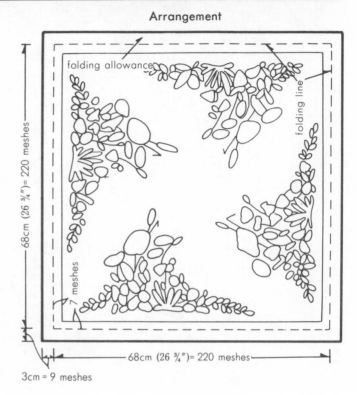

68cm (26 ¾″)= 220 meshes

68cm (26 ¾″) = 220 meshes

3cm = 9 meshes

● Runner

Materials: 64cm by 28cm (25 ¼″ × 11″) Zweigart art. 3706 Stern-Aida [10cm (4″) square = 54 square meshes] ; DMC six-strand embroidery floss No.25: 2 skeins each of Parakeet green (905, 907), 1 skein each of Peacock green (991, 992), Emerald green (911, 954), Pistachio green (368), Tangerine yellow (740), Turkey red (321), Geranium red (350), Poppy (666), Umber gold (977), Buttercup yellow (444), (445), White, Scabious violet (327), Plum (554), Parma violet (209, 211), Mahogany (400), Cerise (601), Soft pink (899, 776), Royal blue (797), Cornflower blue (792), Foget-me-not blue (826), Black (310) and Ash gray (318, 415), a little of Tangerine yellow (742).

Finished size: 59cm by 23cm (23 ¼″ × 9″).

Instructions: After matching the center of pattern and fabric as shown,

cross stitch with 4 strands of floss and line stitch with 3 strands. Pattern A is same as part A of TABLE CENTER.

After completing design, turn back allowance and hand-stitch. Miter corners.

Arrangement

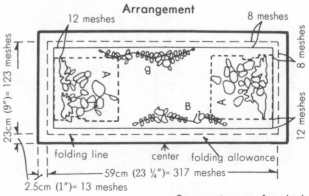

12 meshes

8 meshes

8 meshes

23cm (9″)= 123 meshes

12 meshes

folding line   center   folding allowance

59cm (23 ¼″)= 317 meshes

2.5cm (1″)= 13 meshes

See next page for design.

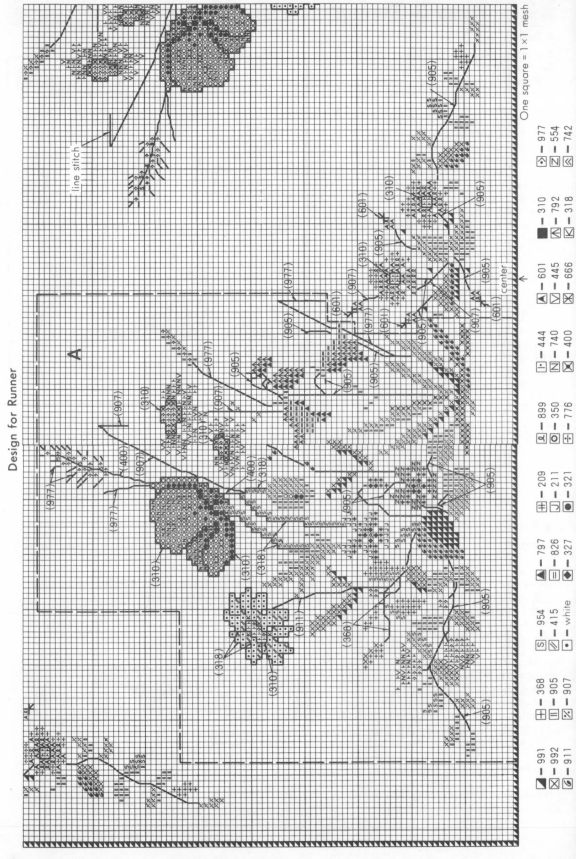

Design for Runner

line stitch

A

center

One square = 1×1 mesh

◨ — 977	◪ — 310	◤ — 601
◈ — 554	◪ — 792	▽ — 445
◩ — 742	◪ — 318	◆ — 666

⊡ — 444	◲ — 899	⊞ — 209
▬ — 740	◎ — 350	◩ — 211
◪ — 400	⊞ — 776	◉ — 321

◀ — 797	◩ — 368	◥ — 991
▥ — 826	⊞ — 905	◪ — 992
◆ — 327	◪ — 907	◪ — 911

◪ — 954	
◪ — 415	
• — white	

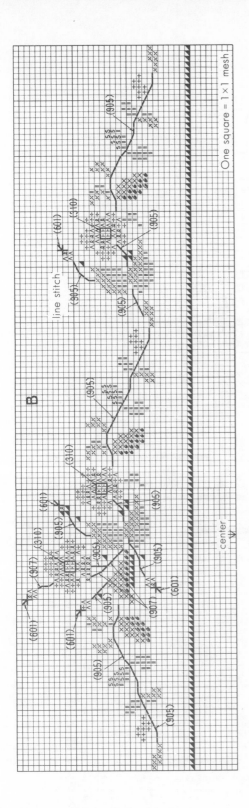

One square = 1×1 mesh

line stitch

B

center

(905) (310) (601) (905) (905) (905) (905) (310) (601) (905) (310) (905) (905) (907) (905) (601) (601) (905) (907) (601) (601) (905) (905)

Picture

Shown on page 26.

Materials: 38cm by 29cm (15″×11 ⅜″) Beige Zweigart art.3706 Stern-Aida [10cm (4″) square = 54 meshes square]; DMC six-strand embroidery floss No. 25: 1 skein each of Scarab green (3345, 3348), Parakeet green (905, 907), Moss green (472), Brilliant green (703), Yellow green (734, 732), Forget-me-not blue (828, 813), Black (310) and White, a little each of Buttercup yellow (444), Lemon yellow (445), Beaver gray (647), Ash gray (413), Beige (3023), Copper green (832), Beige brown (839) and Geranium red (349); Picture frame.

Finished size: See chart.

Instructions: After matching center of pattern and fabric, embroider using 3 strands for cross and half cross stitches and 2 strands for line stitch.

Frame design when finished.

Finished Diagram

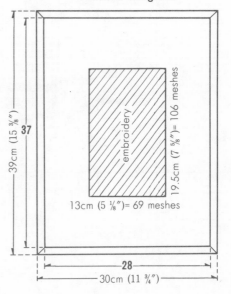

39cm (15 ⅜″) 37

30cm (11 ¾″) 28

embroidery

19.5cm (7 ⅝″)= 106 meshes

13cm (5 ⅛″)= 69 meshes

See next page for design.

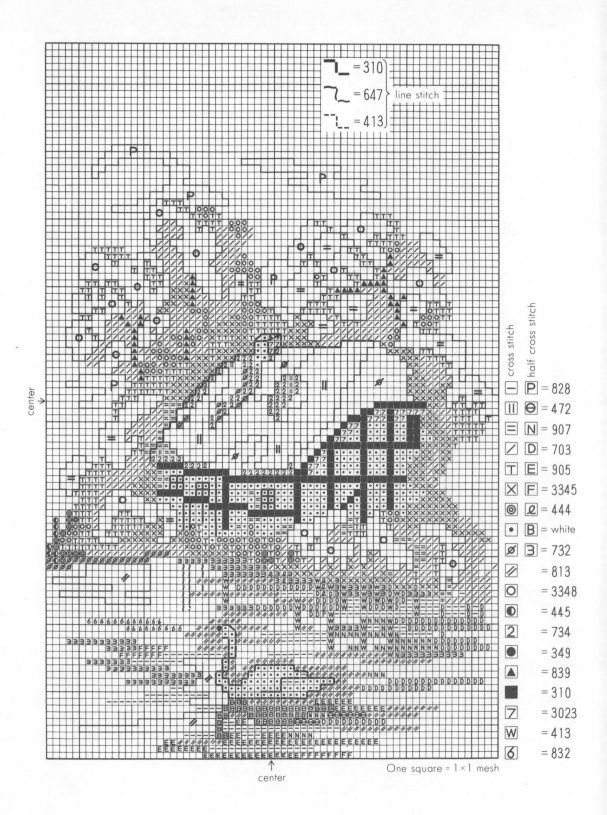

cross stitch | half cross stitch

⊐⌐ = 310 ⎫	
⌐⌐ = 647 ⎬ line stitch	
⌐⌐ = 413 ⎭	

⊟	P	=	828
‖	Θ	=	472
⊜	N	=	907
⁄	D	=	703
T	E	=	905
X	F	=	3345
◎	ℒ	=	444
•	B	=	white
∅	ℨ	=	732
⫽		=	813
O		=	3348
◑		=	445
2		=	734
●		=	349
▲		=	839
■		=	310
7		=	3023
W		=	413
6		=	832

center →

↑ center

One square = 1×1 mesh

50

Materials: 90cm by 40cm (35 ⅜″×15 ¾″) Beige Zweigart art.3707 Hertarette [10cm (4″) square = 32. 5 meshes square] ; DMC six-strand embroidery floss No.25: 2 skeins of Laurel green (986), 1 skein each of Pistachio green (320), Parakeet green (905, 907), Umber (435, 437), Tangerine yellow (743, 745), Geranium red (349, 351, 352, 754), Scarlet (498) and Parma violet (208, 209, 211), a little of Tangerin yellow (742).

Finished size: 40cm by 34cm (15 ¾″×13 ⅜″).

Instructions: Embroider using 8 strands of floss, following chart below. After completing design, have work made into album by specialist.

Arrangement

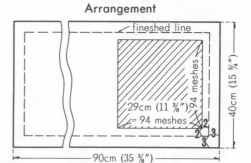

center

center

One square = 1×1 mesh

T =320 ● =986 O =745 ✕ =437 ■ =435 L =907 ◑ =905 S =743 ◪ =742

⊡ =754 ⊘ =352 ③ =351 ▲ =498 ② =349 ⊟ =211 △ =209 ⊞ =208

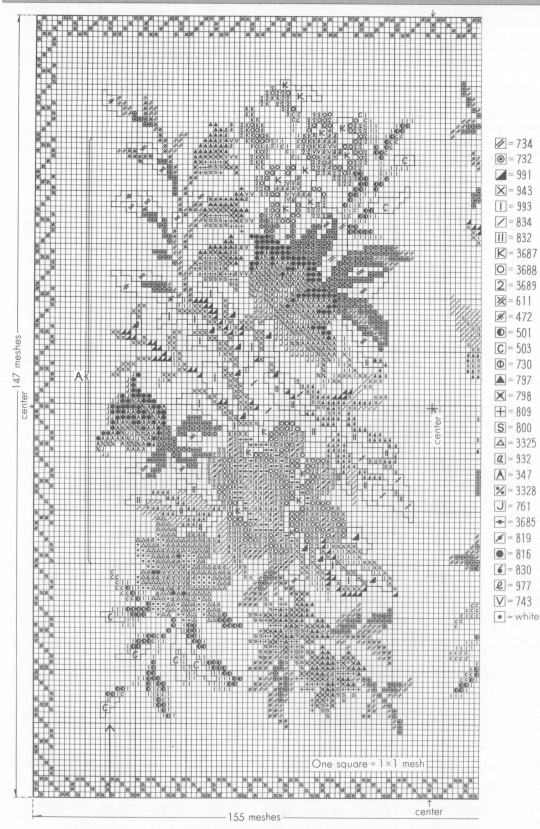

147 meshes

center

center

155 meshes

center

One square = 1×1 mesh

◩ = 734
◉ = 732
◪ = 991
✕ = 943
𝟙 = 993
⧄ = 834
⧚ = 832
K = 3687
O = 3688
2 = 3689
✕ = 611
✗ = 472
◐ = 501
C = 503
◐ = 730
▲ = 797
✕ = 798
✛ = 809
S = 800
△ = 3325
𝒶 = 932
▲ = 347
% = 3328
J = 761
● = 3685
⬗ = 819
● = 816
6 = 830
ℓ = 977
V = 743
• = white

52

Materials: 54cm by 52cm (21 ¼″×20 ½″) Beige Zweigart art.3707 Hertarette〔10cm (4″) square = 32. 5 meshes square〕; DMC six-strand embroidery floss No.25: 3 skeins of Yellow green (734), 2 skeins each of Yellow green (732, 991, 943, 993), Copper green (832, 834), Raspberry red (3687, 3688, 3689) and Drab (611), 1 skein each of Moss green (472), Ivy green (501), Almond green (503), Yellow green (730), Royal blue (797), Sèvres blue (798, 800), Forget-me-not blue (809), Azure blue (3325), Antique blue (932), Cardinal red (347), Morocco red (3328, 761), Raspberry red (3685), Soft pink (819), Scarlet (816) and Copper green (830), a little of Umber gold (977) and Tangerine yellow (743); 54cm by 52cm (19 ¼″×20 ½″) Beige velvet; 46cm (18 ⅛″) long zipper; 100 by 54cm (39 ⅜″×21 ¼″) cotton fabric for inner bag; 400g (14 oz) Polyester fiberfill.

Finished size: 50cm by 48cm (19 ⅝″×18 ⅞″).

Instructions: After cutting out fabric, match centers of material and pattern, and embroider with six strands of floss. Make inner bag 3cm (1 ⅛″) larger than finished size, and stuff with fiberfill.

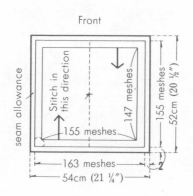

Front

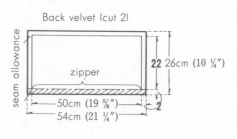

Back velvet (cut 2)

Cushion ——————————— Shown on page 2.

Materials: 96cm by 47cm (37 ¾″×18 ½″) Beige Zweigart art.3707 Hertarette〔10cm (4″) square = 32. 5 meshes square〕; DMC six-strand embroidery floss No.25: 4 skeins of Drab (611), 3 skeins each of Peacock green (993) and Yellow green (734), 2 skeins each of Peacock green (991), Jade green (943), Almond green (503), Copper green (832, 834), Yellow green (732), Moss green (472) and Raspberry red (3687, 3688, 3689), a little each of Raspberry red (3685), Soft pink (819), Cardinal red (347), Morocco red (3328, 761), Royal blue (797), Sèvres blue (798, 800), Forget-me-not blue (809), Azure blue (3325), Antique blue (932), Copper green (830), Yellow green (730), Ivy green (501), Umber gold (977), Tangerine yellow (743), Scarlet (816) and White; 96cm by 50cm (37 ¾″×19 ⅝″) Beige velvet; 50cm (20″) long zipper; 100cm by 105cm (39 ⅜″×41 ⅜″) cotton fabric for inner bag; 970g (34oz) polyester fiberfill.

Finished size: 92cm by 42.5cm (36 ¼″×16 ¾″).

Instructions: After cutting out fabric, embroider with 6 strands, following directions for part A of pattern for cushion. Make inner bag 3cm (1 ⅛″) larger than finished size, and stuff with fiberfill.

Front   Back velvet (cut 2)

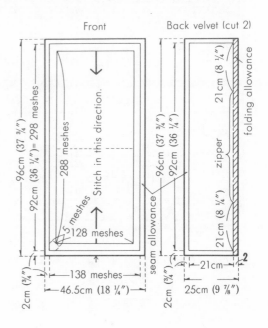

See next page for design.

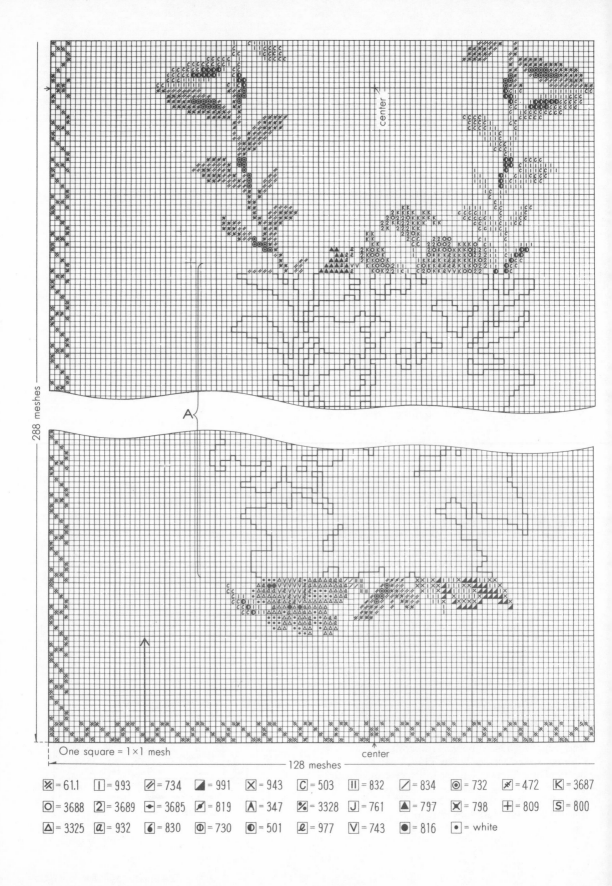

288 meshes

center

center

One square = 1×1 mesh

128 meshes

⊠ = 61.1	I = 993	⊘ = 734	◢ = 991	⊠ = 943	C = 503
⊙ = 3688	② = 3689	☞ = 3685	⊘ = 819	Ⓐ = 347	⊠ = 3328
△ = 3325	ⓐ = 932	⑥ = 830	⊙ = 730	◖ = 501	ℓ = 977

Ⅲ = 832	⊘ = 834	⊙ = 732	✕ = 472	K = 3687
J = 761	▲ = 797	⊠ = 798	+ = 809	S = 800
V = 743	● = 816	• = white		

54

Jewel Box ──────────── Shown on page 21.

Materials: 23cm by 15cm (9″×5 ⅞″) Beige Zweigart art.3706 Stern-Aida [10cm (4″) square = 54 square meshes]; DMC six-strand embroidery floss No.25: one skein each of Smoke gray (640, 642, 644), 0.5 skeins each of Peacock green (993), Jade green (943), Royal blue (995, 996), Geranium pink (891, 894), Tangerine yellow (741), Buttercup yellow (444) and Scarlet (304), a little each of Flame red (608), Canary yellow (972), Plum (552), Parma violet (209), Episcopal purple (915) and Black (310).

Finished size: See chart.

Instructions: Embroider using 3 strands of floss referring to chart. After completing design, have work blocked by specialist.

Arrangement

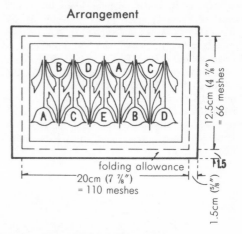

12.5cm (4 ⅞″) = 66 meshes

folding allowance

1.5

20cm (7 ⅞″) = 110 meshes

1.5cm (⅝″)

chain stitch on each mesh

center

One square = 1×1 mesh

center

◉=304	◪=644	◪=552	⊓=996	⊘=891	◉=741
☒·◦=640	⊞=310	∨=209	○=943	⌀=894	∟=444
Ⓢ=642	✳=972	•=995	⟋=993	⫽=608	⊕=915

55

Doily ——————— Shown on page 20.

Materials: 60cm (23 ⅝″) square of Beige Zweigart art.3706 Stern-Aida [10cm (4″) square = 54 square meshes] ; DMC six-strand embroidery floss No.25: 12 skeins of Parakeet green (906), 5 skeins of Scarab green (3345), 4 skeins of Drab (613), 2 skeins each of Royal blue (797), Sèvres blue (799), Plum (554, 552), Canary yellow (971, 973), Cerise (601, 603), Raspberry red (3687, 3689) and Parakeet green (905), a little each of Drab (612) and Black (310).
Finished size: See chart.
Instructions: Cross stitch using 4 strands and chain stitch with 3 strands, as directed on chart. After completing design, turn back allowance, and slip stitch to finish.

● =3345 ○ =797 ⊞ =310 ◢ =552
✕ =906 ◪ =799 ◉ =613 ▽ =554
⊕ =971 ⊘ =603 ⊠ =3687 ◎ =612
⊡ =973 ▨ =601 ⊤ =3689 ⑧ =905

One square = 1×1 mesh

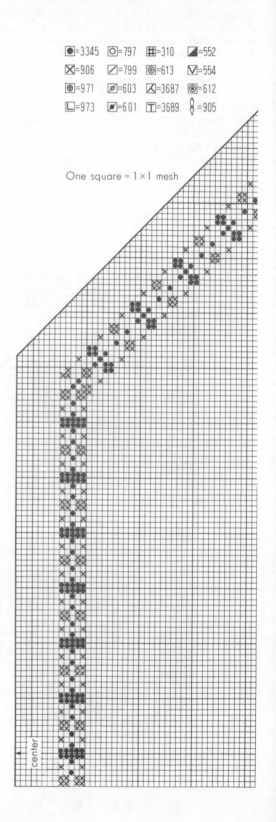

Arrangement

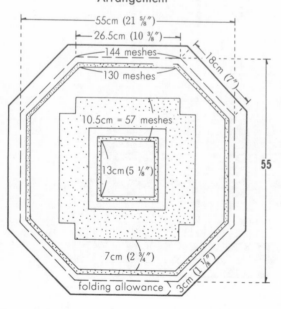

55cm (21 ⅝″)
26.5cm (10 ⅜″)
144 meshes
130 meshes
18cm (7″)
10.5cm = 57 meshes
13cm (5 ⅛″)
55
7cm (2 ¾″)
3cm (1 ⅛″)
folding allowance
center

144 meshes

center

130 meshes

Chain Stitch

38 meshes

chain stitch
on each mesh

70 meshes

70 meshes

center

center

57

⊠=840	Ⅲ=602	◿=727	⊟=733	⏣=841	Ｊ=471
●=632	⌀=603	☰=209	⟩=732	•=644	
Ⅱ=776	Ⅴ=600	⊞=792	▲=935	•.=818	
Ｏ=335	Ｔ=976	Ｚ=798	◹=3012	⊏=745	
Ｓ=3350	⟩=725	◢=3685	Φ=3011	Ʌ=211	

One square = 1×1 mesh

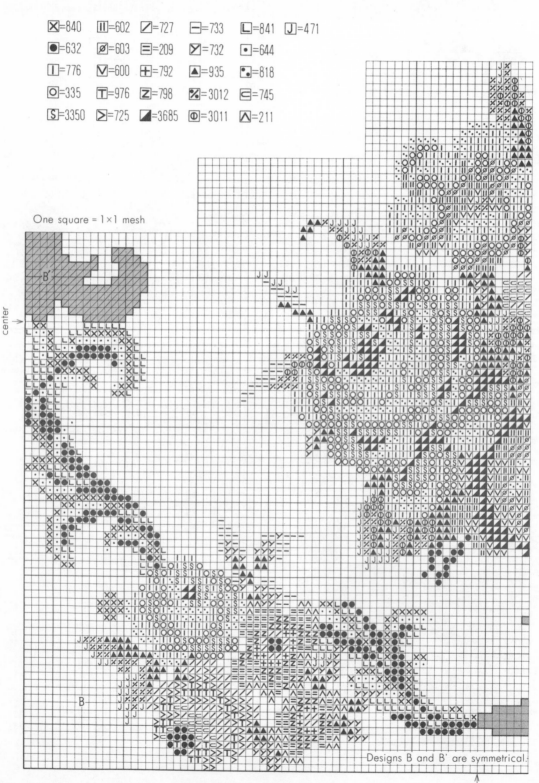

center →

center ↑

Designs B and B' are symmetrical.

Materials: For one cushion: 49cm by 100cm (19 ¼″ × 39 ⅜″) Beige Zweigart art.3707 Hertarette [10cm (4″) square = 32.5 square meshes] ; DMC six-strand embroidery floss No.25: 3 skeins each of Smoke gray (644), Beige brown (840, 841) and Chocolate (632), 2 skeins each of Moss green (935, 471), Yellow green (732, 733), Sage green (3011), Garnet red (335) and Soft pink (776, 818), one skein each of Cerise (600, 602, 603), Raspberry red (3685), Old rose (3350), Parma violet (209, 211), Cornflower blue (792), Sèvres blue (798), Umber gold (976), Saffron (725, 727), Tangerine yellow (745) and Sage green (3012); 100cm by 54cm (39 ⅜″ × 21 ¼″) cotton for inner bag; 90cm by 20cm (35 ⅜″ × 7 ⅞″) Mustard color cotton satin; 8 strands of 190cm (75″) heavy yarns; 45cm (17 ¾″) zipper; 470g (1 lb) polyester fiberfill.

Finished size: 46cm (18 ⅛″) square.

Instructions: Cross stitch with 8 strands and line stitch with 4 strands, according to Chart. After completing design, sew with right sides together, and sew zipper onto center of Back. Sew four pieces of materials for pipe-cord, and run 8 strands of yarns through cord to gather to 190cm (74 ¾″). Stitch cord firmly around cushion. Stuff inner bag, 51cm (20″) square, with fiberfill and assemble cushion.

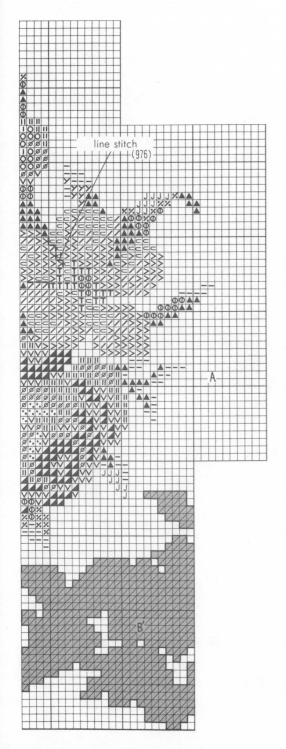

line stitch
(976)

A

B'

Arrangement

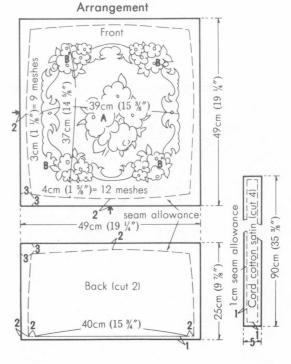

Front

3cm (1 ⅛″) = 9 meshes

37cm (14 ⅝″)

39cm (15 ⅜″)

A

B

B

B

B

49cm (19 ¼″)

4cm (1 ⅝″) = 12 meshes

2 seam allowance

49cm (19 ¼″)

Back (cut 2)

40cm (15 ¾″)

25cm (9 ⅞″)

1cm seam allowance

Cord cotton satin (cut 4)

90cm (35 ⅜″)

Breadbasket Mat ——— Shown on page 23.

Materials: 32cm (12 ⅝″) square White Zweigart art. 3706 Stern-Aida [10cm (4″) square = 54 meshes square] ; DMC six-strand embroidery floss No.25: one skein each of Moss green (937, 472) and Ash gray (415), 0.5 skeins each of Scarab green (3348), Laurel green (986, 989), Canary yellow (972), Saffron (725, 727), Cerise (601, 603, 605), Parma violet (210, 211) and Umber (435), a little of Plum (553); 100cm (39 ⅜″) scroll braid; 102cm long White bias tape of 2cm (¾″) wide.

Finished size: 30.5cm (12″) diameter.

Instructions: After matching pattern and fabric, use 2 strands for line stitch and 4 strands for other stitches. After completing embroidery, cut out fabric in 30cm-diameter circle. Slip stitch after binding scroll braid around doily.

Arrangement

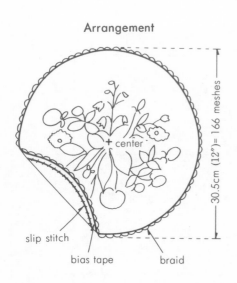

30.5cm (12″)= 166 meshes

slip stitch

bias tape   braid

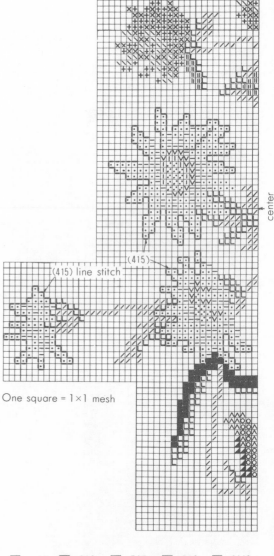

center

(415)

(415) line stitch

One square = 1×1 mesh

⋅=white	■=986	⊡=727	∧=210	‖‖=3348
⌐=937	⊿=989	✕=601	O=211	
⁄=472	V=972	✛=603	●=435	
⊟=415	▯=725	⊠=605	◣=553	

(972)

line stitch
(415)

center

(725)

line stitch
double-cross stitch

line stitch
(725)

One square = 1 x 1 mesh

L = 937	I = 743	X = 601
/ = 3347	X = 745	+ = 603
• = white	◢ = 553	\ = 605
◉ = 435	△ = 210	▲ = 319
− = 415	O = 211	II = 472
V = 972		

Chart A

line stitch

(972)

(318)

(318)

(318)

line stitch

center
48meshes

Chart B

(318)

(318)

(318)

center

Wall Hanging —————————— Shown on page 22.

Materials: 66cm by 18cm (26″ by 7 $\frac{1}{16}$″) Beige Zweigart art.3706 Stern-Aida [10cm (4″) square = 54 meshes square]; DMC six-strand embroidery floss No. 25: 2 skeins each of Moss green (937) and Scarab green (3347), 1 skein each of White, Umber (435), Ash gray (318, 415), Canary yellow (972), Tangerine yellow (745, 743), Plum (553), Parma violet (210, 211), Cerise (601, 603, 605), Pistachio green (319) and Moss green (472); 60cm by 14cm (23 $\frac{5}{8}$″ × 5 $\frac{1}{2}$″) cotton fabric for lining; one pair of metal bars for hanging. (See picture.)

Finished size: See chart.

Instructions: Following chart, cross stitch with 4 strands and line stitch with 3 strands. After completing design, line the work with cotton, and secure metal bars on both upper and lower edges. (See finished diagram.)

Arrangement

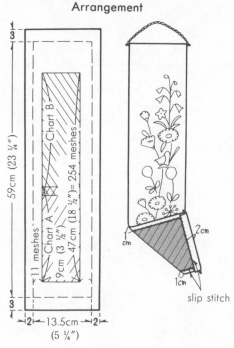

Design on the left page.

Album —————————— Shown on page 32.

Materials: 90cm by 39cm (35 $\frac{3}{8}$″ × 15 $\frac{3}{8}$″) Beige Zweigart art.3706 Stern-Aida [10cm (4″) square = 54 meshes square]; DMC six-strand embroidery floss No. 25: 1.5 skeins each of Drab (612) and Moss green (472), 1 skein each of Copper green (830), Old gold (676), Green (3051) and Scarlet (815), 0.5 skeins each of Seagull gray (451, 452, 453, 3072), Copper green (832), Peacock green (991, 992, 993), Scarab green (3345, 3347), Sage green (3012, 3013), Green (3053), Pistachio green (320), Jade green (943), Yellow green (734), Garnet red (309), Soft pink (776), Peony rose (956), Raspberry red (3685, 3687, 3688, 3689), Old gold (680, 729), Drab (613), Smoke gray (644), Ivy green (501, 502), Lemon yellow (445), Light yellow (3078), Canary yellow (970, 972, 973), Scarlet (498, 304), Parakeet green (906), Flame red (606) and White.

Finished size: 40cm by 33cm (15 $\frac{3}{4}$″ × 13″).

Instructions: Embroider with 4 strands on marked area as shown on chart. After completing design, have it blocked by specialist.

Arrangement

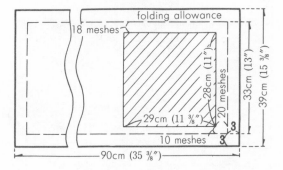

63

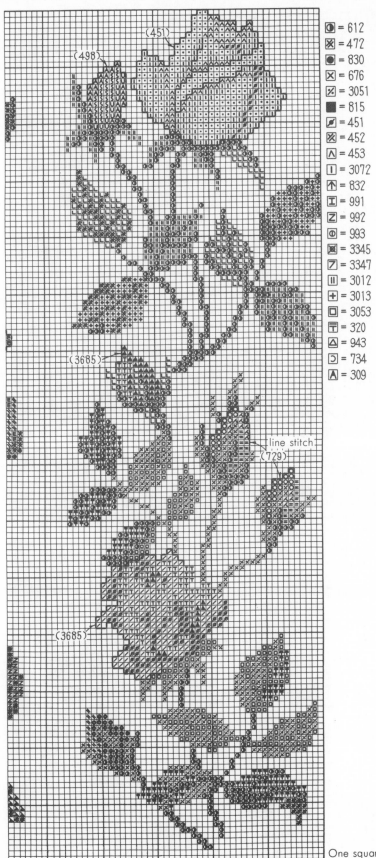

◖ = 612	ⓢ = 776
⊠ = 472	Ⓤ = 956
◕ = 830	▲ = 3685
⊠ = 676	Ⓣ = 3687
⊠ = 3051	◪ = 3688
■ = 815	◿ = 3689
◢ = 451	◎ = 680
⊠ = 452	⊟ = 729
∧ = 453	⌴ = 613
Ⅱ = 3072	⊠ = 644
⬆ = 832	⊗ = 501
Ⅰ = 991	◣ = 502
Ⅱ = 992	Ｏ = 445
⏀ = 993	⊩ = 3078
⊠ = 3345	◎ = 970
◿ = 3347	◨ = 972
‖ = 3012	Ｅ = 973
⊞ = 3013	⊘ = 498
▭ = 3053	▲ = 304
Ⓣ = 320	ⓢ = 906
△ = 943	◪ = 606
⅃ = 734	• = white
Ａ = 309	

line stitch (729)

One square = 1×1 mesh

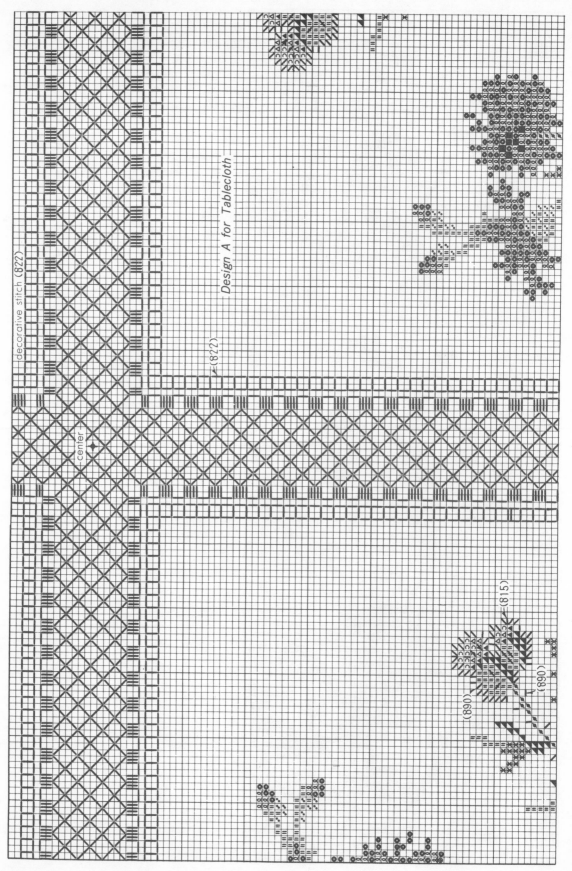

decorative stitch (822)

Design A for Tablecloth

center

=(822)

=(815)

(890)

(890)

66

decorative stitch

(844)

(844)

(844)

(844)

67 squares (134 meshes)

center

(890)

(815)

(890)

(890)

(972)

(844)

64 squares (128 meshes)

(815)

(890)

(844)

(844)

67

center

(972)

(844)

Design B

(890)

(890)

(815)

(815)

(815)

(890)

(890)

(890)

Tablecloth ——————— Shown on page 14.

Materials: 140cm (55 ⅛″) square Beige Zweigart art. 3947 Oslo [10cm (4″) square = 87 meshes square] ; DMC six-strand embroidery floss No.25: 7 skeins of Scarab green (3347), 5 skeins each of Scarab green (3345) and Smoke gray (822), 4 skeins of White, 2 skeins each of Golden green (580), Beaver gray (844) and Geranium red (350), 1 skein each of Pistachio green (320, 890), Scarlet (815), Geranium red (817),

Directions for Decorative Stitch

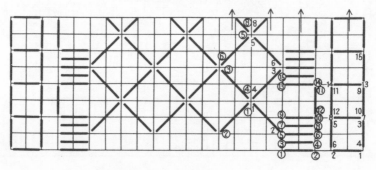

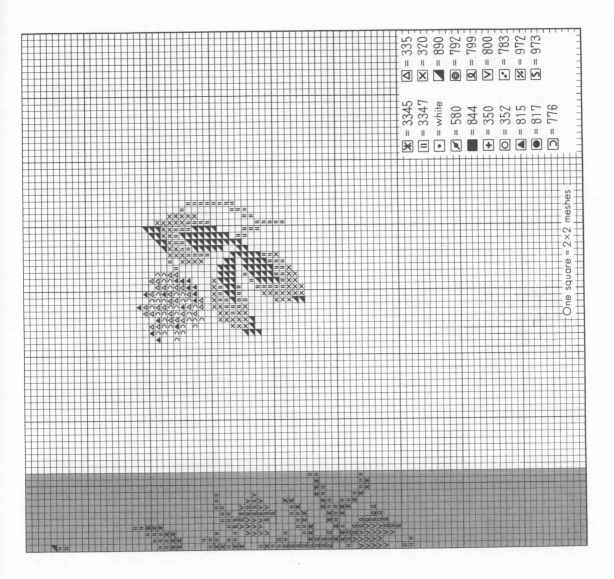

◁ = 335	✕ = 320	◣ = 890	◎ = 792	◨ = 799	▽ = 800	⊡ = 783	✖ = 972	⑤ = 973	
✖ = 3345	⹀ = 3347	• = white	◥ = 580	■ = 844	✚ = 350	○ = 352	◀ = 815	● = 817	⌒ = 776

One square = 2×2 meshes

Soft pink (776), Geranium red (352), Garnet red
(335), Cornflower blue (792), Sèvres blue (799, 800),
Golden yellow (783) and Canary yellow (972, 973).
Finished size: 125cm (49 ¼″) square.
Instructions: After matching centers of fabric and
pattern, cross stitch with 4 strands and line stitch
with 2 strands, as shown in picture. Follow directions to make decorative stitches. After completing design, pull out 2 fabric yarns 4cm (1 ⅝″) in
from finished line and make half hem stitches.
Miter each corner.

Designs shown on pages 66-69

Arrangement

134 meshes   128 meshes

folding allowance

128 meshes

134 meshes

Design A

center

Design B

128 meshes   134 meshes

half-hem stitch   38cm (15″)= 330 meshes

140cm (55 ⅛″)

140cm (55 ⅛″)

7.5

7.5

Materials TABLE CENTER: 83cm by 35cm (32 ⅝″ ×13 ¾″) Beige Zweigart art.3706 Stern-Aida [10cm (4″) square = 54 meshes square] ; DMC six-strand embroidery floss No.25: 2 skeins of Copper green (830), 1 skein each of Scarlet (816), Geranium red (817, 350, 352), Saffron (725, 726), Umber gold (976), Indigo (334), Sky blue (517, 519), Moss green (935), Ivy green (501), Yellow green (733), Sage green (3013), Black (310) and White.

TRAY MAT: 34cm by 20cm (13 ⅜″×7 ⅞″) Beige Zweigart art.3609 Belfast [10cm (4″) square = 122 meshes square] ; DMC six-strand embroider floss No. 25: one skein each of Geranium red (350, 352, 817), Scarlet (498), Saffron (725, 727), Golden yellow (782), Sky blue (517, 519), Copper green (829, 831), Yellow green (730, 733), Black (310), White and # 25 Cotton à broder Beige.

Finished size TABLE CENTER: 77cm by 29cm (30 ⅜″×11 ⅜″).

TRAY MAT: 34cm by 20cm (13 ⅜″×7 ⅞″).

Instructions: Cross stitch with 3 strands, line stitch with 2 strands, and closed-buttonhole stitch with one strand, according to chart. After completing table center design, turn back allowance, and miter each corner. Cut out tray mat, and closed-buttonhole stitch around edges.

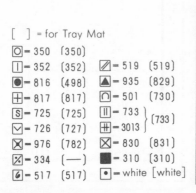

[ ] = for Tray Mat

O = 350 (350)				
I = 352 (352)		⊿ = 519 (519)		
● = 816 (498)		▲ = 935 (829)		
+ = 817 (817)		∩ = 501 (730)		
S = 725 (725)		II = 733 ⎫ (733)		
∨ = 726 (727)		⊞ = 3013 ⎭		
X = 976 (782)		⊠ = 830 (831)		
⊠ = 334 (—)		■ = 310 (310)		
6 = 517 (517)		⊡ = white [white]		

= for Tray Mat

line stitch

725
725
725
725
725
725
725
976
976
976
976

519
519

310

501
(730)

501
(730)

501
(730)

center — 184 meshes

center

24cm (9 ½")= 129 meshes.

center

226 meshes

24cm (9 ½") = 129 meshes

One square = 2×2 meshes

One square = 1×1 mesh

Runner

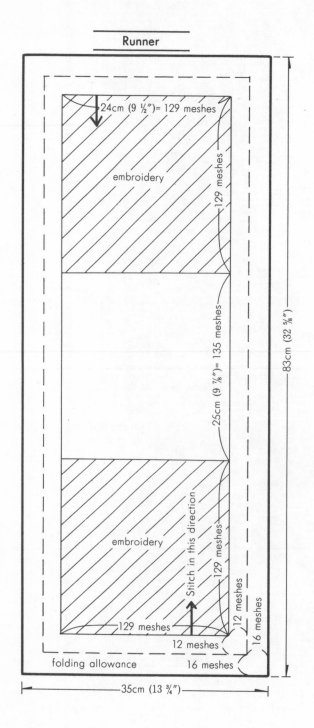

24cm (9 ½") = 129 meshes

embroidery

129 meshes

25cm (9 ⅞") = 135 meshes

83cm (32 ⅝")

embroidery

Stitch in this direction

129 meshes

129 meshes

12 meshes

16 meshes

12 meshes

16 meshes

folding allowance

35cm (13 ¾")

Tray Mat

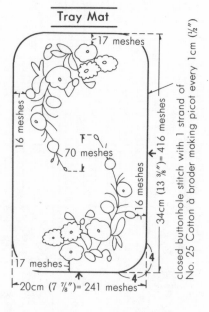

17 meshes

16 meshes

70 meshes

34cm (13 ⅜") = 416 meshes

16 meshes

16 meshes

17 meshes

20cm (7 ⅞") = 241 meshes

4

4

closed buttonhole stitch with 1 strand of
No. 25 Cotton à broder making picot every 1cm (½")

Directions for picot, see page 45.

Materials: 75cm by 135cm (29 ½″×53 ⅛″) Beige Zweigart art.3706 Stern-Aida [10cm (4″) square = 54 meshes square] ; DMC six-strand embroidery floss No.25: 5 skeins of Parakeet green (905), 4 skeins each of Scabious violet (327), Geranium pink (894), Parakeet green (907), 3 skeins each of Parma violet (209, 211), Geranium red (817, 892), Tangerine yellow (742, 740), Saffron (726), Yellow green (731) and Drab (610, 612), 2 skeins of Moss green (472), 1 skein of Coffee brown (801), a little of Umber (434, 436).

Finished size: 66cm by 125cm (26″×49 ¼″).

Instructions: After matching centers of pattern and fabric, cross stitch with 4 strands and line stitch with 2 strands. Embroidery of 100th to 181st squares should be done symmetrically to that of 16th to 87th squares. Turn under edges twice and half hem stitch.

Arrangement

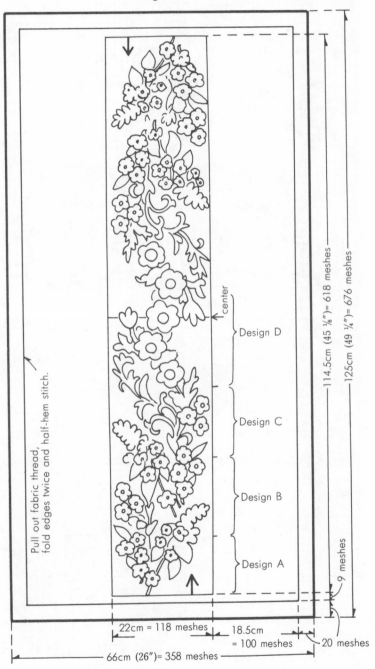

Pull out fabric thread, fold edges twice and half-hem stitch.

center

Design D

Design C

Design B

Design A

114.5cm (45 ⅛″)= 618 meshes

125cm (49 ¼″)= 676 meshes

9 meshes

20 meshes

22cm = 118 meshes

18.5cm = 100 meshes

66cm (26″)= 358 meshes

Designs on pages 74-77.

73

Design B

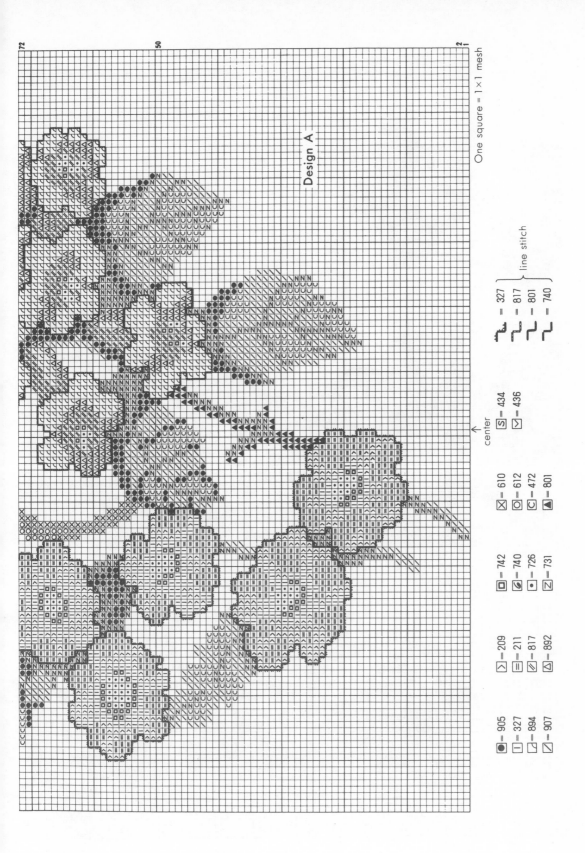

Design A

One square = 1×1 mesh

line stitch

⌐ = 327
⌐ = 817
⌐ = 801
⌐ = 740

center

S = 434	X = 610	∨ = 209	● = 905
∨ = 436	O = 612	≡ = 211	⊡ = 327
	⌐ = 472	⊘ = 817	⊠ = 894
	▲ = 801	△ = 892	⊿ = 907
	⊡ = 742		
	◪ = 740		
	• = 726		
	∑ = 731		

75

Design D

Design C

Album

Shown on page 31.

Materials: 88cm by 40cm (34 ⅝″ × 15 ¾″) Beige Zweigart art.3706 Stern-Aida [10cm (4″) square = 54 square meshes] ; DMC six-strand embroidery floss No.25: 2 skeins each of Soft pink (899) and Moss green (469, 471), 1 skein each of White, Seagull gray (3072), Soft pink (776), Garnet red (326), Geranium red (817), Flame red (606, 608), Scarlet (902), Canary yellow (972), Buttercup yellow (444), Lemon yellow (445), Scabious violet (327), Parma violet (208, 210), Pistachio green (368), Laurel green (988) and Moss green (936, 472).

Finished size: 40cm by 33.5cm (15 ¾″ ×13 ¼″).

Instructions: Embroider with 4 strands, according to chart. After completing design, ask specialist to make work into album.

Arrangement

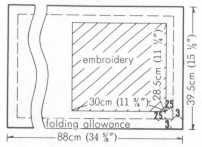

embroidery

30cm (11 ¾″)

28.5cm (11 ¼″)

39.5cm (15 ½″)

25

7.5 3

3

folding allowance

88cm (34 ⅝″)

U = 899	✦ = 972
⊠ = 469	N = 444
V = 471	L = 445
•·ɑ = white	● = 327
╱ = 3072	△ = 208
= = 776	⊞ = 210
S = 326	O = 368
⦂ = 817	T = 988
Ⅲ = 606	■ = 936
⊠ = 608	⊡ = 472
◪ = 902	

center

One square = 1×1 mesh

center

Materials: 85cm by 44cm (33 ½″ × 17 ⅜″) Beige Zweigart art.3707 Hertarette [10cm (4″) square = 32.5 meshes square]; DMC six-strand embroidery floss No. 25: 4 skeins of Golden yellow (780), 3 skeins of Coffee brown (801), 2 skeins each of Scarab green (3345, 3347), one skein each of Golden yellow (783), Saffron (725, 727), Geranium red (351, 754, 353, 349), Cardinal red (347), Scarab green (3346, 3348), Peacock green (991, 993), Emerald green (955), Azure blue (3325) and Indigo (334); 34cm (13 ⅜″) long Zipper; 100cm by 50cm (39 ⅜″ × 19 ⅝″) cotton fabric for Inner bag; 440g (1 lb) Polyester fiberfill.

Finished size: 41cm (16 ⅛″) square.

Instructions: After cutting out material according to chart, match centers of pattern and fabric. Cross stitch with 8 strands and line stitch with 4 strands. Leave space open in center of back side for zipper (See diagram). Inner should be made 3cm (1 ⅛″) larger than finished size.

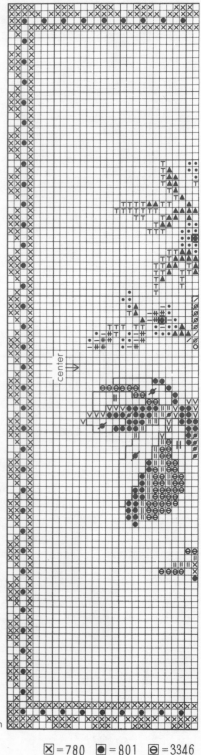

Arrangement

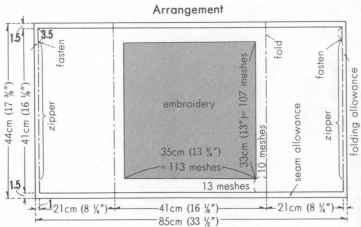

One square = 1×1 mesh

$\boxtimes$ = 780 $\boxedbullet$ = 801 $\ominus$ = 3346

$\varobslash$ = 347 $\boxplus$ = 349 $\boxed{\text{I}}$ = 995

center

| | | = 3347 | ☑ = 783 | S = 725 | Ⓞ = 351 | ☑ = 754 | △ = 727 | ☑ = 353 | ㄱ = 801 |
| | | | | | | | | ㄱ = 349 ⎫ line stitch |

☑ = 3345   V = 3348   ▲ = 991   T = 993   ⊟ = 3325   ⊞ = 334   • = white   ꓼ = 754

Materials: 86cm by 30cm (33 ⅞″×11 ¾″) Beige
Zweigart art.3706 Stern-Aida [10cm (4″) square = 54
meshes] ; DMC six-strand embroidery floss No.25: 4
skeins of Scarab green (3345),3 skeins each of Geranium red (817), Brilliant green (703), 2 skeins each of
Flame red (606, 608) and Parakeet green (907), 1 skein
of Moss green (469), Umber (433), a little each of
Canary yellow (973) and Saffron (727).

Finished size: 80cm by 24cm (31 ½″×9 ½″).
Instructions: After matching the center of fabric and
pattern, cross stitch with 4 strands, line stitch with 1
strand of (907) and 3 strands of (433). After completing design, turn back folding allowance, and miter
corners to finish.

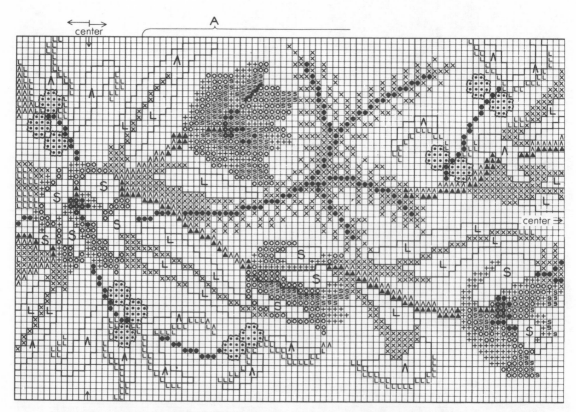

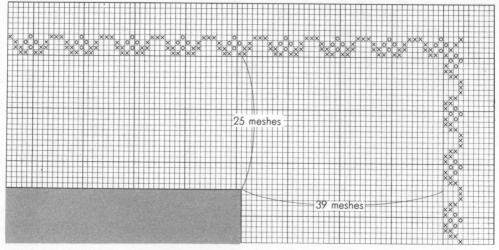

Arrangement

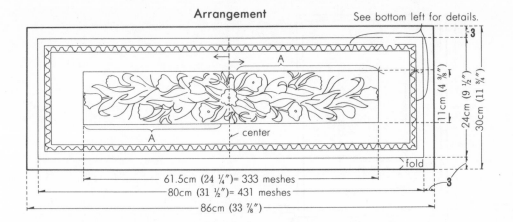

See bottom left for details.

center

A

A

fold

11cm (4 ³⁄₈")

24cm (9 ½")

30cm (11 ¾")

3

3

61.5cm (24 ¼")= 333 meshes

80cm (31 ½")= 431 meshes

86cm (33 ⅞")

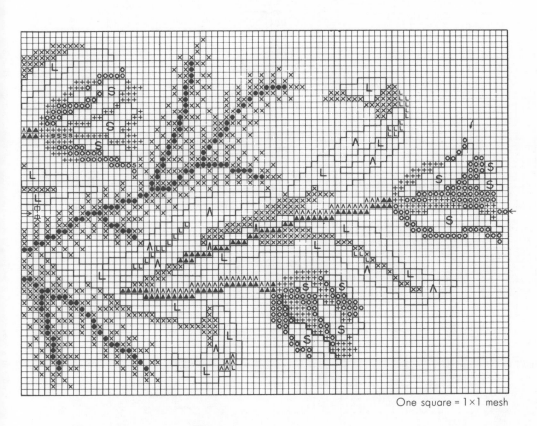

One square = 1×1 mesh

☒ = 3345

➕ = 817

🄻 = 703

🅂 = 608

🄾 = 606

⋀ = 907

▲ = 469

● = 433

◉ = 973

• = 727

⌐ = 433
⌐ = 907 } line stitch

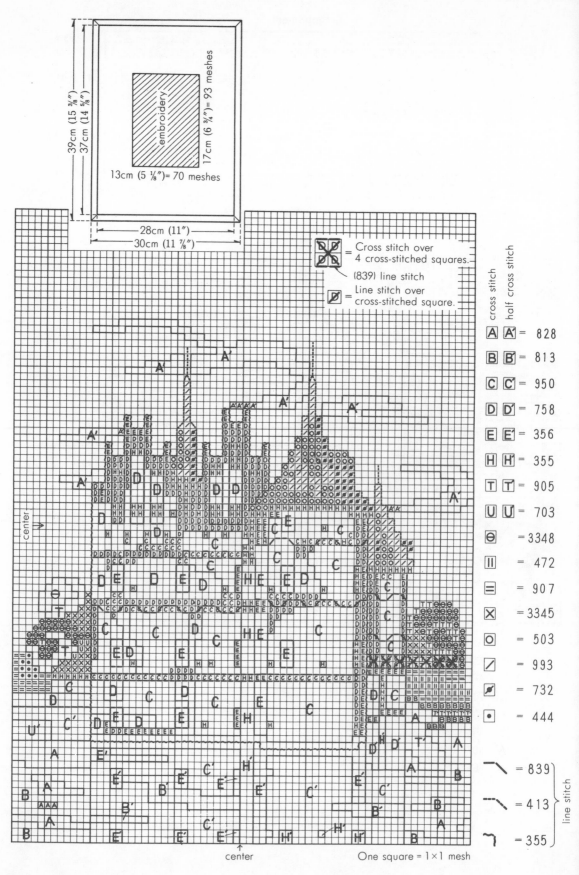

embroidery

39cm (15 3/8")
37cm (14 5/8")

17cm (6 3/4") = 93 meshes
13cm (5 1/8") = 70 meshes

28cm (11")
30cm (11 7/8")

= Cross stitch over
4 cross-stitched squares.

(839) line stitch

= Line stitch over
cross-stitched square.

cross stitch
half cross stitch

A	A'	= 828
B	B'	= 813
C	C'	= 950
D	D'	= 758
E	E'	= 356
H	H'	= 355
T	T'	= 905
U	U'	= 703
Θ		= 3348
II		= 472
=		= 907
X		= 3345
O		= 503
/		= 993
⌀		= 732
•		= 444

= 839
= 413   line stitch
= 355

center

center

One square = 1×1 mesh

84

Picture ——————————— Shown on page 28.

Materials: 38cm by 28cm (15″ × 11″) Beige Zweigart art.3706 Stern-Aida [10cm (4″) square = 54 meshes] ; DMC six-strand embroidery floss No.25: 1 skein each of Forget-me-not blue (813, 828), Scarab green (3348, 3345), Moss green (472), Parakeet green (905, 907), Brilliant green (703), Almond green (503), Peacock green (993), Yellow green (732), Chestnut (950), Terra-cotta (355, 356, 758) and Beige brown (839), a little each of Buttercup yellow (444) and Ash gray (413); Picture frame.

Finished size: See chart.
Instructions: After matching centers of pattern and fabric, cross stitch with 3 strands and line stitch with 2 strands. Frame completed work.

Picture ——————————— Shown on page 29.

Materials: 38cm by 29cm (15″ × 11 ⅜″) Beige Zweigart art.3706 Stern-Aida [10cm (4″) square = 54 meshes] ; DMC six-strand embroidery floss No.25: 1 skein each of Forget-me-not blue (828, 813), Scarab green (3348, 3345), Brilliant green (703), Parakeet green (905), Almond green (503), Yellow green (732), Terra-cotta (758, 356, 355), Chestnut (407), Beige green (839) and Copper green (832), a little each of Black (310), White, Moss green (472), Parakeet green (907), Peacock green (993), Green (3053), Chestnut (950), Lemon yellow (445), Beige (3023), Beaver gray (647), Ash gray (413) and Old gold (676); Picture frame.

Finished size: See chart.
Instructions: After matching centers of pattern and fabric, use 3 strands each for cross and half cross stitches and use 2 strands for line stitch. Frame embroidery when finished.

See next page for design.

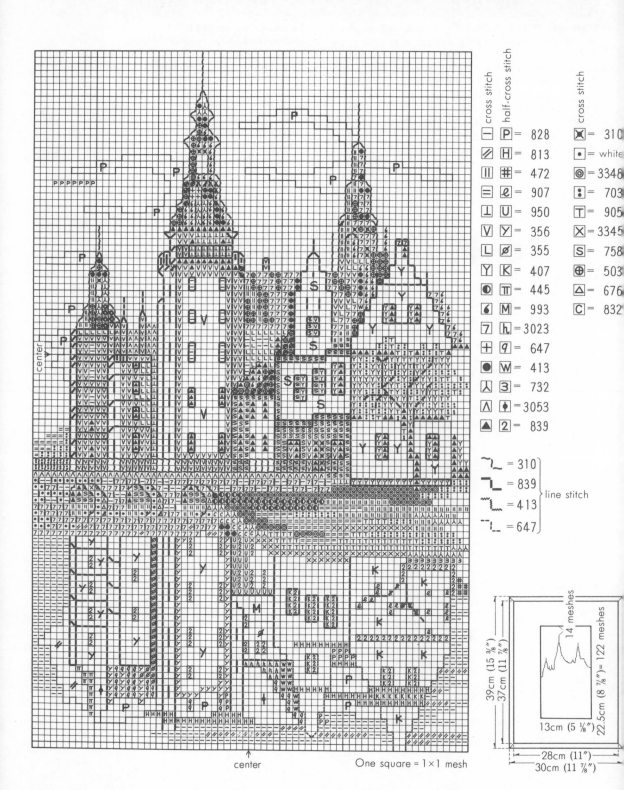

			cross stitch half-cross stitch			cross stitch	
⊟	P	=	828	⊠	=	310
⧄	H	=	813	⊡•	=	white
⫴⫴	⊞	=	472	⊚	=	3348
⊟	ℓ	=	907	⊟•	=	703
⊥	U	=	950	T	=	905
⫴V	Y	=	356	X	=	3345
∟	∅	=	355	S	=	758
Y	K	=	407	⊕	=	503
◐	⫪	=	445	△	=	676
⌀	M	=	993	C	=	832
7	h	=	3023			
⊞	9	=	647			
●	W	=	413			
⅄	3	=	732			
∧	◉	=	3053			
▲	2	=	839			

~⌐ = 310
⌐ = 839 } line stitch
⌁ = 413
-⌐-- = 647

One square = 1×1 mesh

center

39cm (15 ³⁄₈")
37cm (11 ⁷⁄₈")
22.5cm (8 ⁷⁄₈") = 122 meshes
14 meshes
13cm (5 ¹⁄₈")
28cm (11")
30cm (11 ⁷⁄₈")

Basics in Cross-Stitch

Cross-Stitch

In Cross-Stitch, the design is worked regularly by making crosses in the same direction. Use the even-weave fabrics or canvas which you can count the threads easily. You may use a checked fabric like gingham as a guide for Cross-Stitch. Use a blunt needle made for Cross-Stitch with which you can pick up the threads easily. You may use a blunt tapestry needle when working on heavyweight fabrics, wool or knit.

To work horizontally:

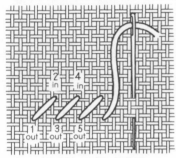

Work across all stitches in each row from left to right.

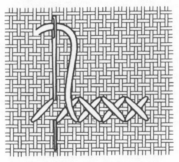

When coming to the end, cross back in the other direction from right to left.

To work downward horizontally:

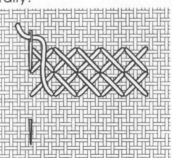

To work upward horizontally:

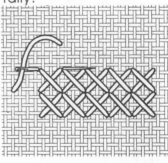

To complete each cross horizontally:

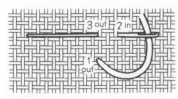

Bring the thread out at the lower left and take a stitch from 2 to 3.

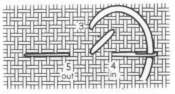

Insert the needle at 4 and take a stitch to 5.

Continue to work, completing each cross.

To complete each cross vertically:

Bring the thread out at the upper right and take a stitch from 2 to 3.

Insert the needle at 4 to form a cross and take a stitch to 5.

Take a stitch from 6 to 7.

Complete each cross working vertically. The direction of the threads must be the same, when working downward or upward.

To work upward diagonally:

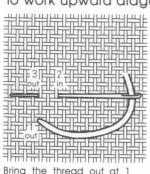 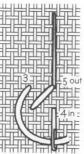 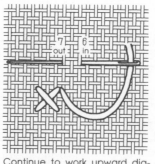 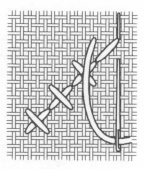

Bring the thread out at 1 and take a horizontal stitch from 2 to 3.

Take a vertical stitch from 4 to 5.

Continue to work upward diagonally, completing each cross.

To work downward diagonally:

 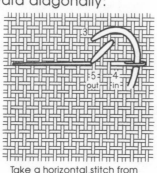  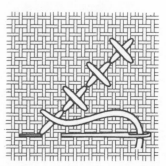

Bring the thread out at 1 and take a vertical stitch from 2 to 3.

Take a horizontal stitch from 4 to 5.

Continue to work downward diagonally, completing each cross.

Overcast the cut-edge before you work.

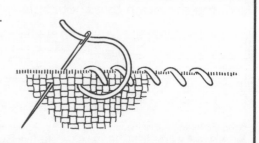

Suitable fabrics for Cross Stitch are easy to fray. Overcast the cut-edge before you start working for easy handling.

Holbein Stitch

This is also called Line Stitch and is sometimes used for outlining or dividing cross-stitched area.

The stitch is completed by running stitches in both ways. Stitches on the wrong side are the same on the front.

Straight Line:

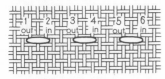

Take stitches of equal length.

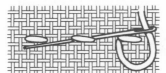

When coming to the end of design, return in the same way filling in the spaces left by the first row. Always insert the needle in the same direction for a neater finish.

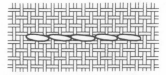

Diagonal Line:

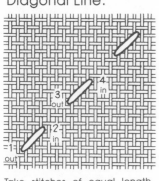

Take stitches of equal length diagonally.

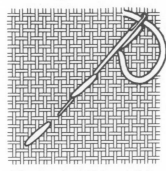

When coming to the end of design, return in the same way as for the Straight Line.

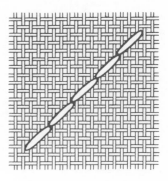

Zigzag Line:

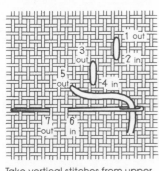

Take vertical stitches from upper right.

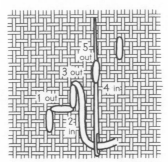

Bring the thread at 1 and take a vertical stitch from 2 to 3.

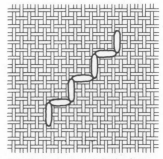

On return journey, take horizontal stitches to make zigzag line.

Double Cross-Stitch

Work Cross-Stitch first. Then work another Cross-Stitch over the previous one. Always bring the needle out and insert it in the same way.

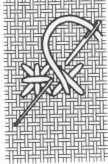

Half Cross-Stitch

One half of the cross or a diagonal stitch is usually called Half Cross-Stitch, but the stitches shown below are called Half Cross-Stitch in this book.

The directions of the stitches are shown as follows.

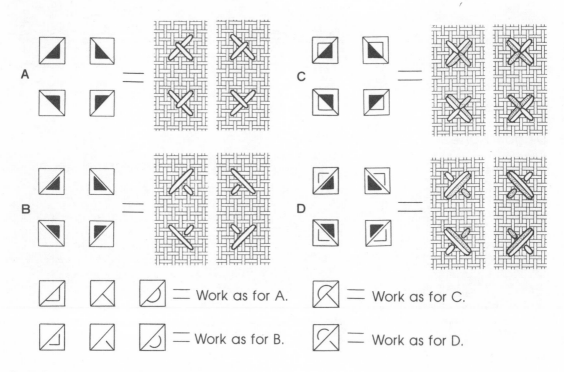

Fabrics, Threads and Needles

Fabrics(actual size)

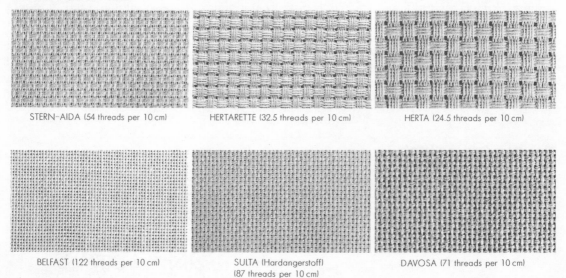

STERN–AIDA (54 threads per 10 cm)

HERTARETTE (32.5 threads per 10 cm)

HERTA (24.5 threads per 10 cm)

BELFAST (122 threads per 10 cm)

SULTA (Hardangerstoff) (87 threads per 10 cm)

DAVOSA (71 threads per 10 cm)

In the Cross-Stitch Embroidery, the designs are worked from charts by counting the threads of the fabric. Use even-weave fabric or canvas whose threads can be counted easily.

The fabrics suited to the Cross-Stitch Embroidery are shown in the photos on the opposite page. Most of them are cotton or linen, but wool, silk or synthetics may be also used depending on its purpose.

Are evenweave fabrics and the most suitable for the Cross-Stitch Embroidery.

DAVOSA . . . Is woven with single thick thread, thus this is a heavy-weight canvas. This is often used for the Cross-Stitch Embroidery and the Free-style Embroidery with bold designs.

SULTA (Hardangerstoff) . . . Is often used for the Counted Thread Embroidery. This is evenly woven with double threads.

evenly woven with double threads.

Even-weave linen ... Light or medium-weight linen is mostly used. Light-weight linen is suitable for making tablecloths with complicated designs.

Counted Thread Embroidery

In the Cross-Stitch Embroidery, the finished size will vary depending on fineness or coarseness of the fabric used. Always check the thread count per inch when buying the fabric.

Threads

A wide variety of threads is available in the market, but choose the most suitable thread for the purpose, the design and the fabric.

Six Strand Floss, No. 25 — One thread consists of 6 strands, and measures 8 m per skein. You can pull out as many threads as required from the bundle if necessary (according to the design).

Pearl Cotton, No. 5 — Single thick thread, and is quite lustrous. One skein measures 25m. Suitable for rough stitches.

Needles

Blunt-pointed needles or tapestry needles are often used for the Counted Thread Embroidery. The needles from No. 19 to No. 23 are suitable for the Cross-Stitch Embroidery. The larger the number, the finer and shorter the needle.

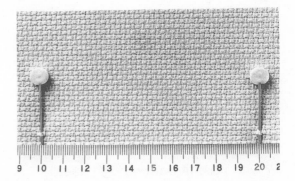

Cotton à broder, No. 4 — Made of four two-ply threads twisted together.

Besides these, you have a wide variety of them such as cottons, rayons, silk, wools ... even metal threads. The sizes also range from thick, medium, fine and extreme fine.

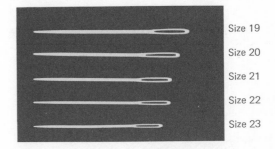

Size 19
Size 20
Size 21
Size 22
Size 23

Effective Combination of Fabric and Thread

The chart on the right shows the ~effective combination of the fabric and the embroidery thread. If the background fabric is shown through the embroidery or if you have a tendency to pull the working thread too tightly, use more strands of the thread in needle.

Fabrics	Gauge (10 cm)	Six strand floss, No. 25
STERN-AIDA	54 threads	3 – 4 strands
HERTARETTE (Medium weight)	32.5 threads	6 strands
HERTA (Heavy weight)	24.5 threads	10 – 12 strands
DAVOSA	71 threads	6 strands
SULTA (Hardangerstoff)	87 threads	4 strands

How to handle thread

The threads Nos. 25, 5 and 4 come in a bundle or ring, depending on the manufacturer. When they are formed in a ring, untie the twist, and cut one end of the ring with scissors, and pull out one by one. When they are gathered together and held by one or two paper labels, pull out the length from the core of the bundle.

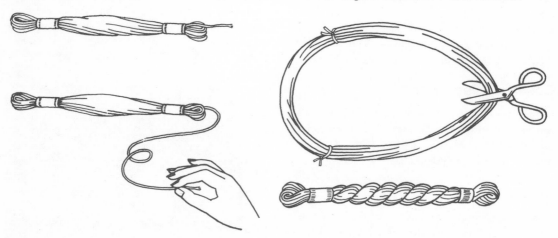

How to pass thread through needle

When you pass 4 strands of the thread through an embroidery needle, fold the ends of the threads, and insert the folded edge through hole of the needle. (See illustration at right) Do the same way when you pass a thick yarn like wool.

Direction of Stitches

All the crosses of the piece should be in the same direction. Always work all the underneath threads in one direction and the top threads in the opposite.

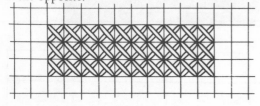

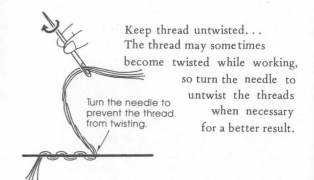

Keep thread untwisted. . .
The thread may sometimes become twisted while working, so turn the needle to untwist the threads when necessary for a better result.

Turn the needle to prevent the thread from twisting.

Length of thread . . . Cut the thread about 50cm long at a time. If you use longer thread, the lust of the thread will be lost and you may have a poor result.

Where to start . . . You may start wherever you like provided that you count the threads and follow the chart properly. However, it is easier to work when starting at center or at the corner of a motif.

Tension of thread . . . Pulling the thread too tightly or too loosely will damage the finished work. Always keep the tension of the thread evenly.

Embroidery hoop . . . You may work cross-stitches without using an embroidery hoop, but it will help keeping even tension of the thread. Be sure to use an embroidery hoop for working Half Cross-Stitch.

How to start

Start embroidery leaving the end of the thread twice as long as the needle to be used. When the embroidery is finished, weave both ends of the thread into the stitches on the wrong side. It is advisable not to make knots at the beginning and ending, for they will show on the front or sometimes come out through the fabric. When using double or even number of strands, fold the thread in half and start working as shown at left.

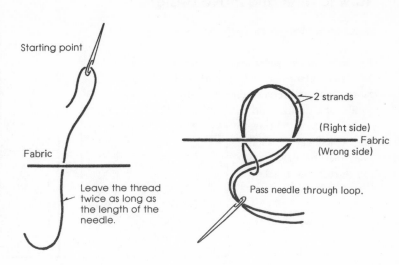

Starting point

Fabric

Leave the thread twice as long as the length of the needle.

2 strands

(Right side)
Fabric
(Wrong side)

Pass needle through loop.

Finishing

Check whether there are any mistakes in the direction of the stitches or any skipped area. Also make sure that the ends of the thread are woven into the stitches and trimmed off neatly.

How to press

Spray water over the wrong side of the embroidered piece. Place a blanket covered with a white cloth on the ironing board. Place the damp embroidered piece on the top with the wrong side up. Press gently stretching the fabric along the grain, then along the selvages.

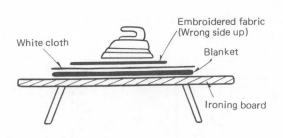

White cloth

Embroidered fabric (Wrong side up)

Blanket

Ironing board

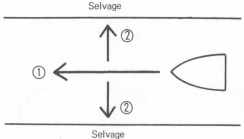

Selvage

①

②

②

Selvage

How to wash

It takes a long time to finish a piece of work and sometimes the fabric and the embroidery thread become soiled from working. If they are washable, wash gently with mild detergent and warm water. Rinse well, dry in the shade and press.

How to alter and make designs

How to enlarge or reduce designs

By using different thread count fabric ... You can enlarge or reduce designs by using a fabric with different thread count. For example, the design worked on Indian cloth (50 threads per 4 inches) is smaller than that on Java canvas (35 threads per 4 inches).

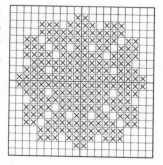

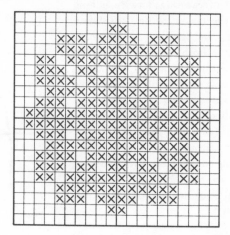

By multiplying the squares of the design ... If the squares of the original design are doubled vertically and horizontally, the enlarged design has 4 by 4 squares. Besides, you can enlarge designs by working one cross over two or three fabric threads.

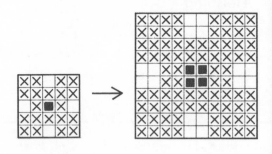

How to make designs for the Cross-Stitch Embroidery

If you want to work from your own design, make a sketch on a graph paper. Then fill the squares according to the original lines. Then color as you desire.

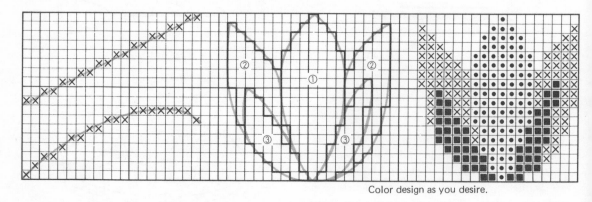

Color design as you desire.

How to work Cross-Stitch without using charts

The Cross-Stitch Embroidery is usually worked from charts, but you can work by following designs transfered on the fabric. First, transfer a design on the fabric using a dressmaker's carbon paper. Then, fill the design with cross-stitches. You can enlarge or reduce designs freely and also can use the same designs made for the Free-style Embroidery.

Edge Finishes

*Slip stitch folding edges twice:

① Fold cut edge about 0.5 cm wide, fold again at the finished line. In case of thick fabric, trim the surplus on the corner.
② Baste steady.
③ Bring needle out on the turned back 0.2 cm off the fold, scoop the other side few woven threads. Repeat scooping the other side at 1 cm intervals.

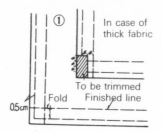

In case of thick fabric

To be trimmed
Finished line
Fold
0.5cm

Baste

Catch stitch :

Used for bulky fabric.
① Turn cut edge, steady with basting.
② Work from left to right. Bring needle out on the turned back right below the cut edge, scoop the other side few woven threads, then scoop the turned back top piece only. Repeat.

Wrong side

Baste

Scoop few woven threads

3 2 7 6
1 5 4

Hemstitching :

① Draw threads out after the cut edges of fabric are straightened.
② Turn cut edge all around twice to wrong side, baste steady, work hemstitching from wrong side.

Drawing threads out :

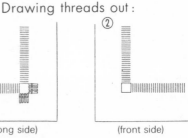

(wrong side)   (front side)

Draw threads out crosswise and lengthwise, stitch edges of threads steady

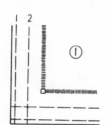
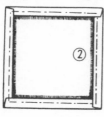

Oneside-hemstitching :

① Pick up few threads passing needle left to right as shown.
② Bring needle out right at the base of following threads, draw the thread on the needle.

Bothsides-hemstitching :

Work oneside-hemstitching on both sides.

Mitering :

① Mark lines on turning as shown with dotted line, trim off the area of oblique lines.
② Turn cut edge following numerical order.
③ Turn 4, 5, baste, finish with slip stitch.

To be trimmed off

4 5
Finished outline
3
2
1
Fold in numerical order

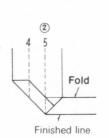

4 5
Fold
Finished line

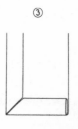